Here Comes Santa Claus

CONTENTS

2	Here Comes Santa Claus (Right Down Santa Claus Lane)
5	A Holly Jolly Christmas
8	It's Beginning to Look Like Christmas
13	Jingle-Bell Rock
18	Merry Christmas, Darling
24	Nuttin' for Christmas
28	Shake Me I Rattle (Squeeze Me I Cry)

ISBN 0-634-06455-X

7777 W. BLUEMOUND RD. P.O. BOX 13819 MILWAUKEE, WI 53213

For all works contained herein:
Unauthorized copying, arranging, adapting, recording or public performance is an infringement of copyright.
Infringers are liable under the law.

Visit Hal Leonard Online at
www.halleonard.com

Here Comes Santa Claus
(Right Down Santa Claus Lane)

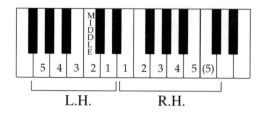

Words and Music by Gene Autry
and Oakley Haldeman

1. Here comes Santa Claus! Here comes Santa Claus!
2. Here comes Santa Claus! Here comes Santa Claus!
3., 4. *(See additional lyrics)*

Right down Santa Claus Lane! Vixen and Blitzen and
Right down Santa Claus Lane! He's got a bag that is

Duet Part (Student plays one octave higher than written.)

© 1947 (Renewed) Gene Autry's Western Music Publishing Co.
All Rights Reserved   Used by Permission

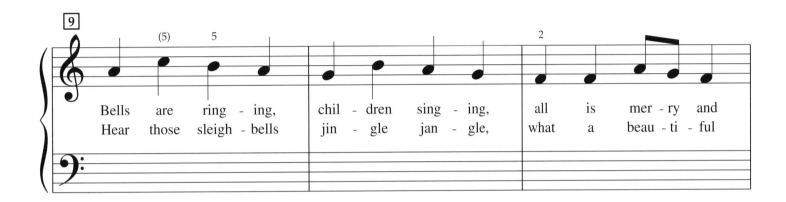
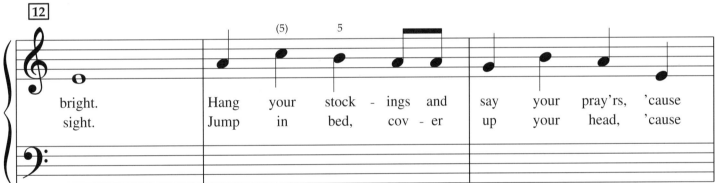

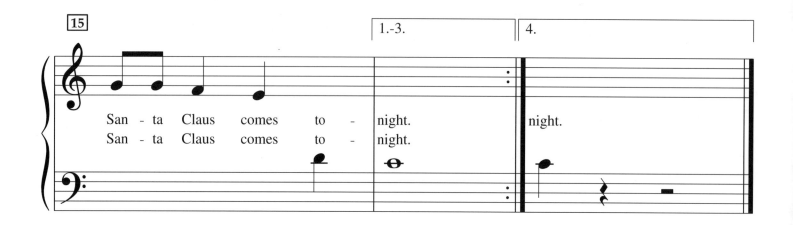

Additional Lyrics

3. Here comes Santa Claus! Here comes Santa Claus!
   Right down Santa Claus Lane!
   He doesn't care if you're rich or poor
   For he loves you just the same.
   Santa knows that we're God's children,
   That makes ev'rything right.
   Fill your hearts with a Christmas cheer,
   'Cause Santa Claus comes tonight.

4. Here comes Santa Claus! Here comes Santa Claus!
   Right down Santa Claus Lane!
   He'll come around when the chimes ring out,
   Then it's Christmas time again.
   Peace on earth will come to all
   If we just follow the light.
   Let's give thanks to the Lord above,
   'Cause Santa Claus comes tonight.

A Holly Jolly Christmas

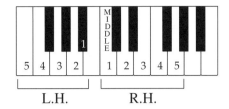
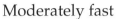

Music and Lyrics by
Johnny Marks

Duet Part (Student plays one octave higher than written.)

Copyright © 1962, 1964 (Renewed 1990, 1992) St. Nicholas Music Inc.,
1619 Broadway, New York, New York 10019
All Rights Reserved

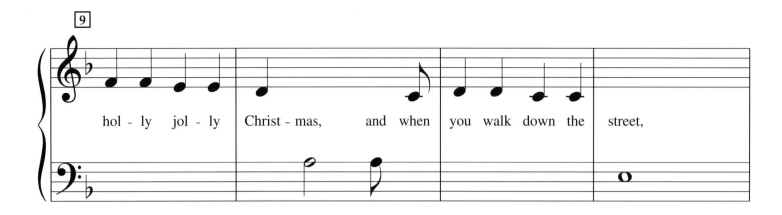
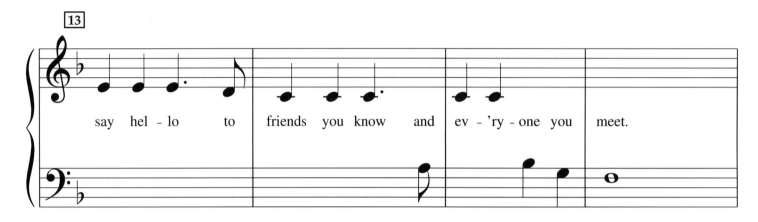
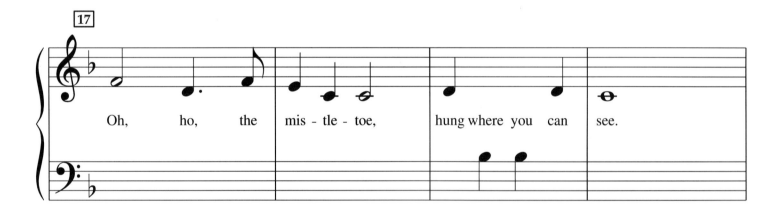
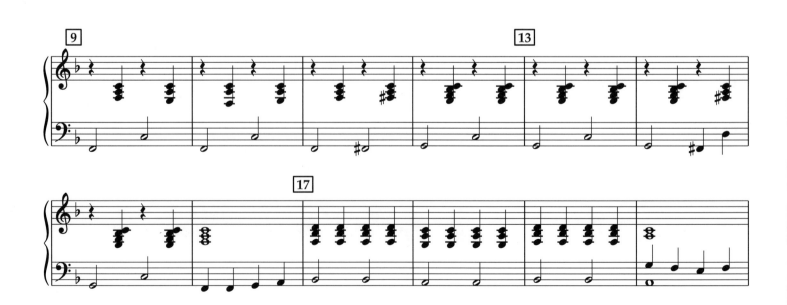

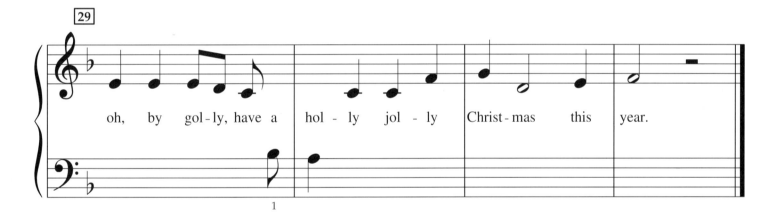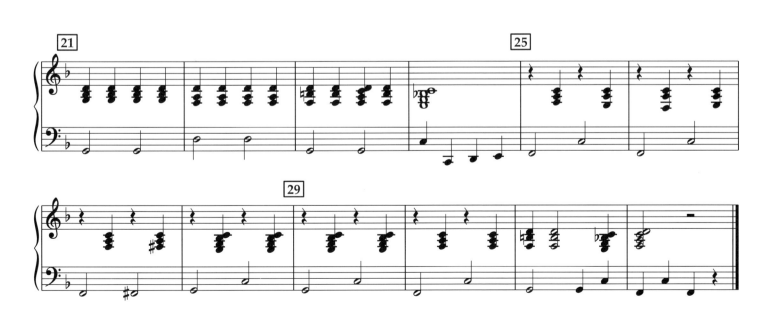

It's Beginning to Look Like Christmas

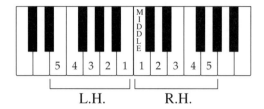

By Meredith Willson

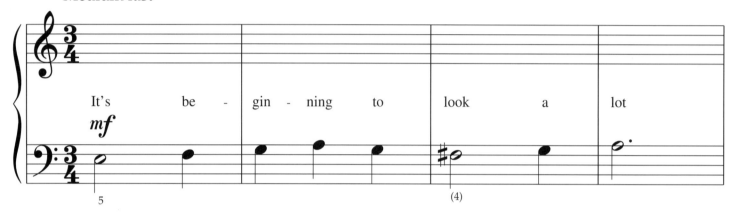

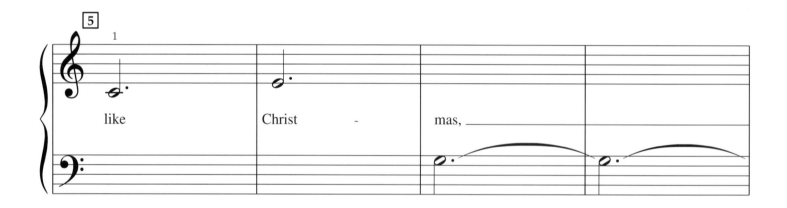

Duet Part (Student plays one octave higher than written.)

© 1951 PLYMOUTH MUSIC CO., INC.
© Renewed 1979 FRANK MUSIC CORP. and MEREDITH WILLSON MUSIC
All Rights Reserved

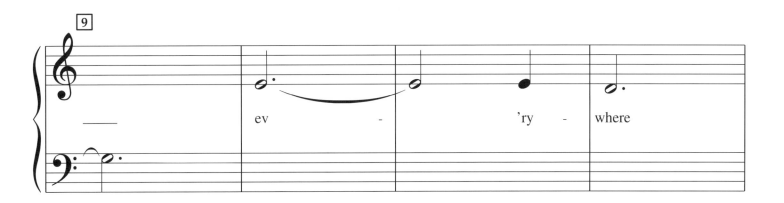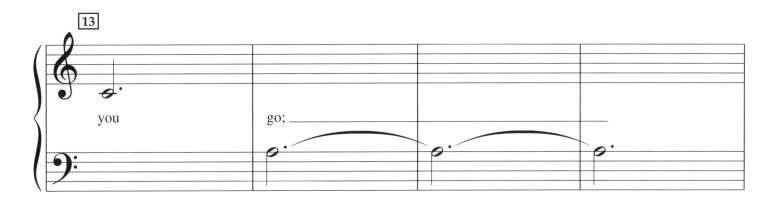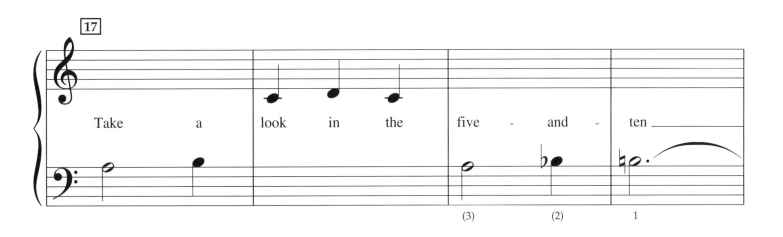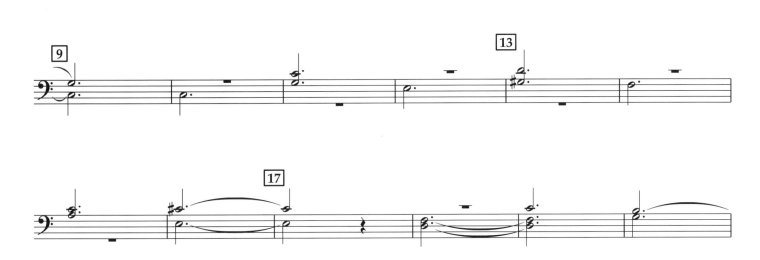

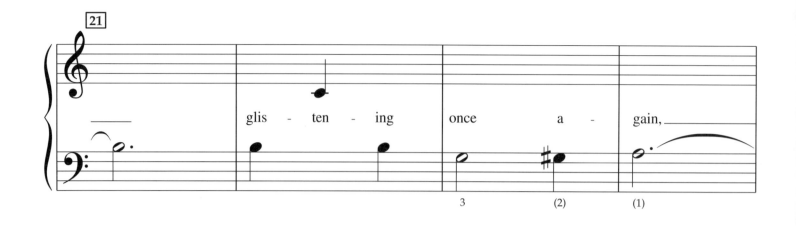
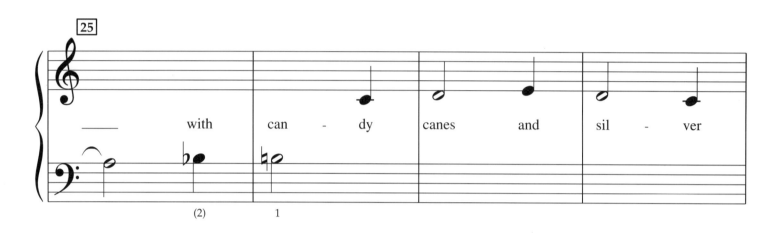

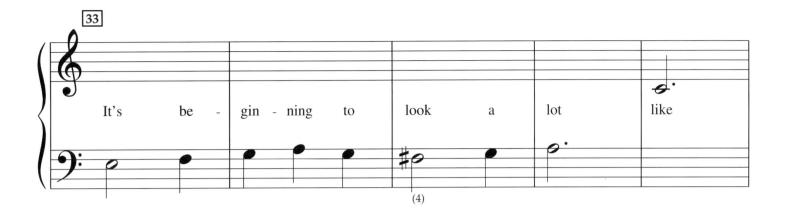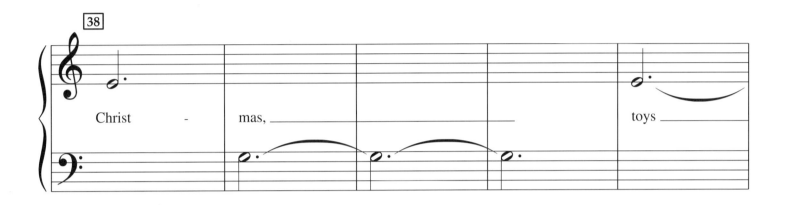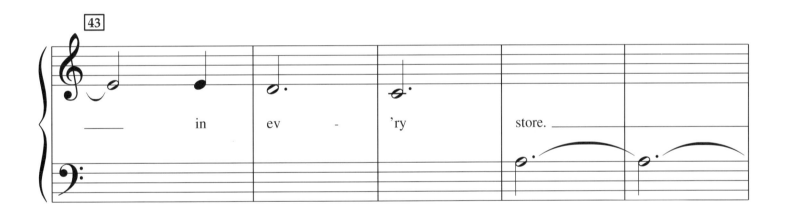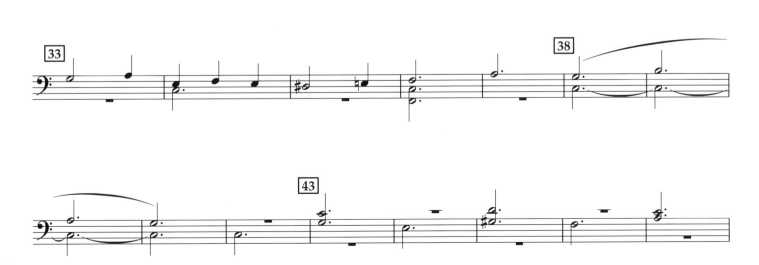

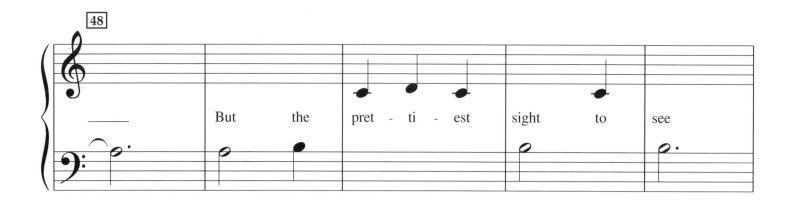
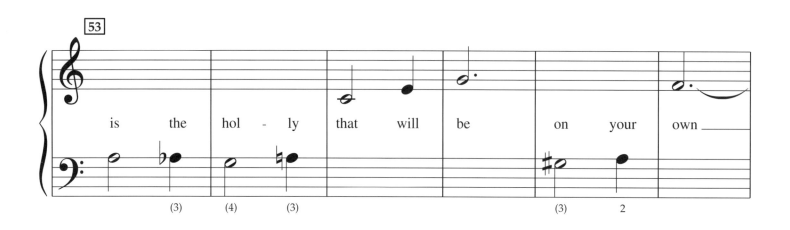

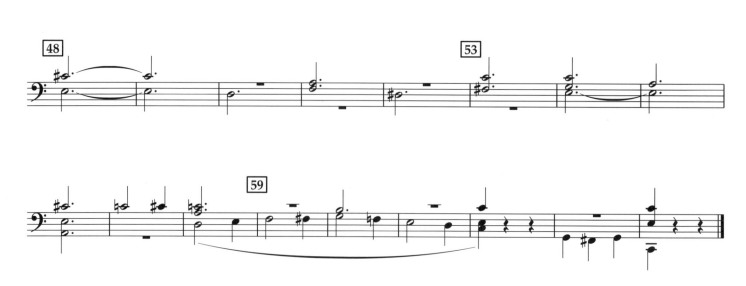

Jingle-Bell Rock

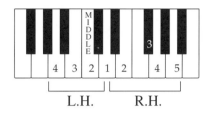

Words and Music by Joe Beal
and Jim Boothe

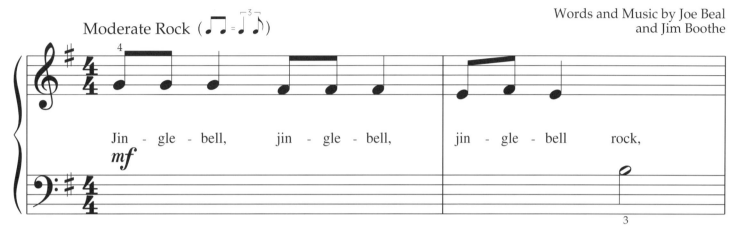

Duet Part (Student plays one octave higher than written.)

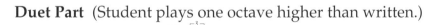

Copyright © 1957 by Chappell & Co.
Copyright Renewed
International Copyright Secured   All Rights Reserved

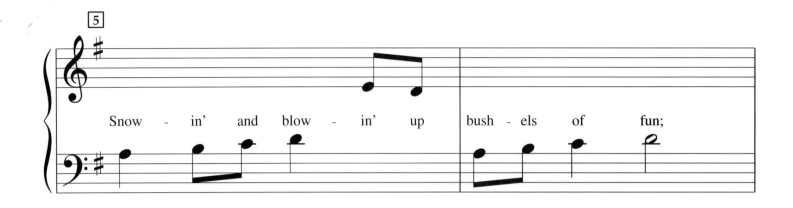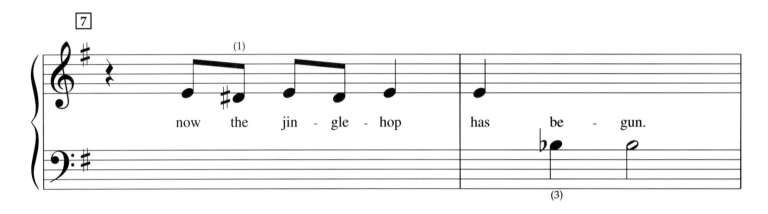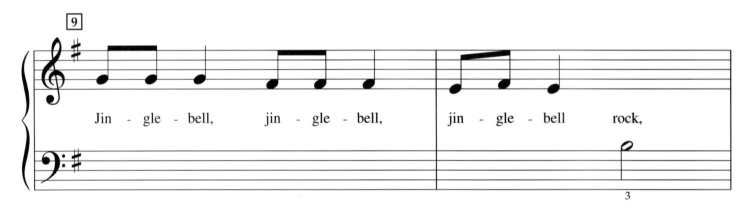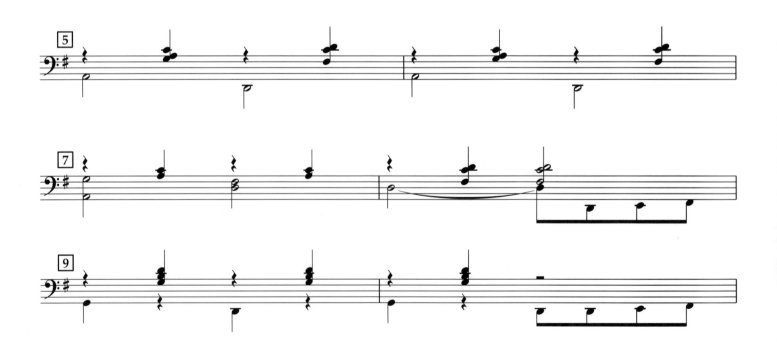

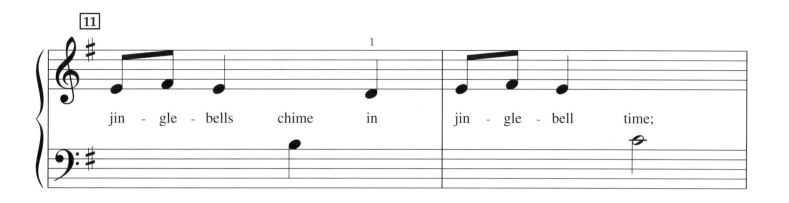
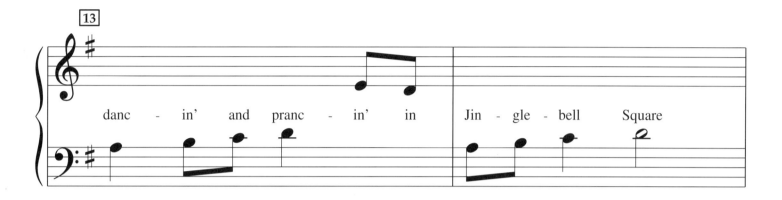

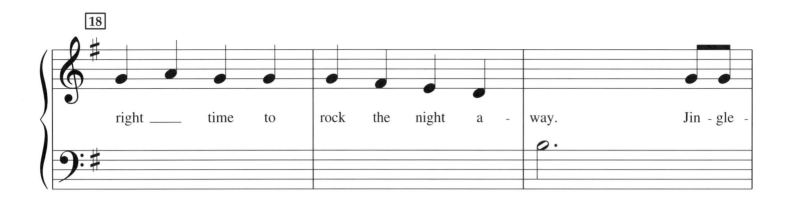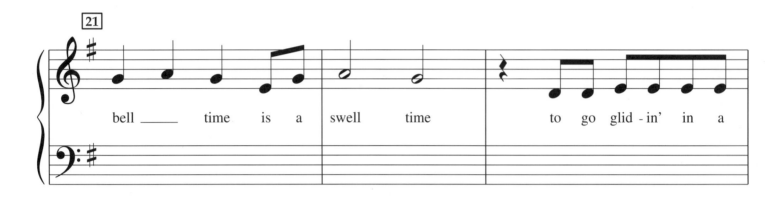

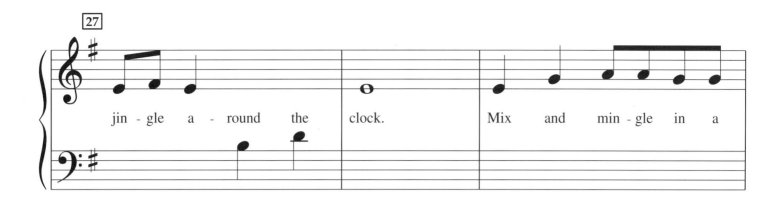

Merry Christmas, Darling

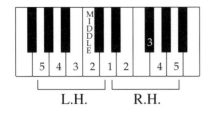

Words and Music by Richard Carpenter
and Frank Pooler

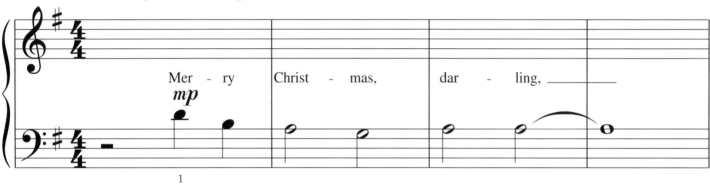

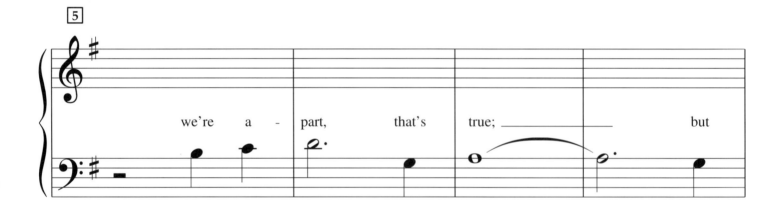

Duet Part (Student plays one octave higher than written.)

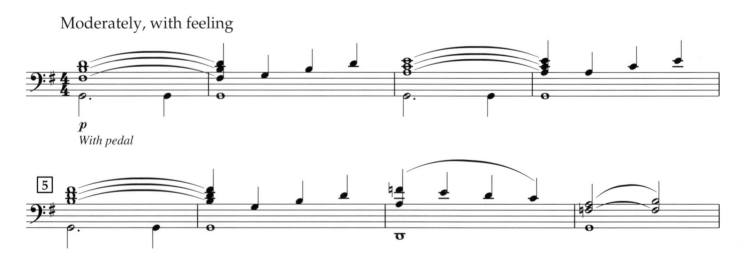

Copyright © 1970 IRVING MUSIC, INC.
Copyright Renewed
All Rights Reserved   Used by Permission

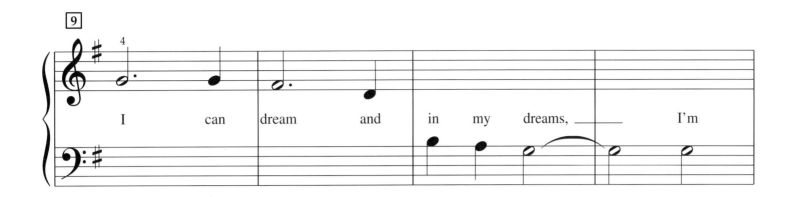
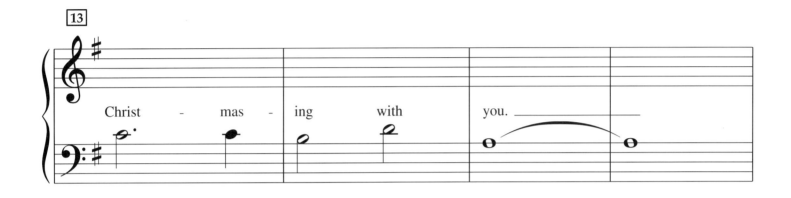
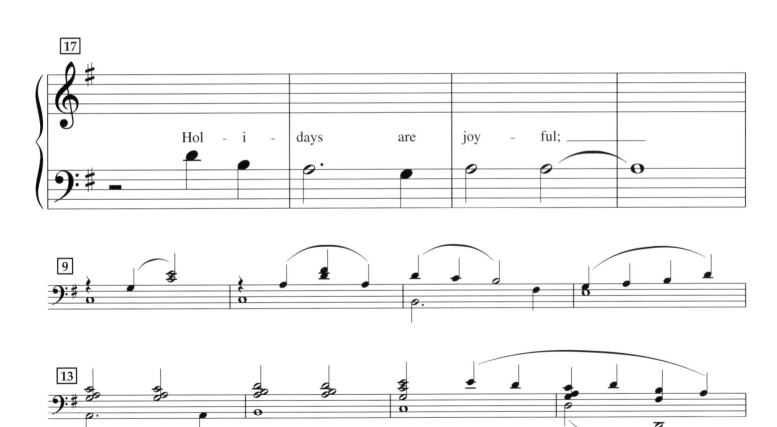
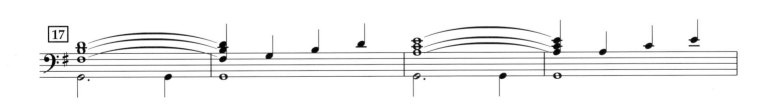

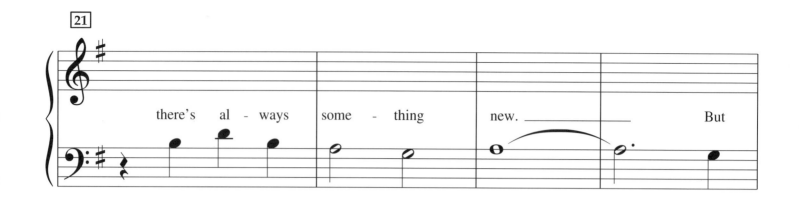
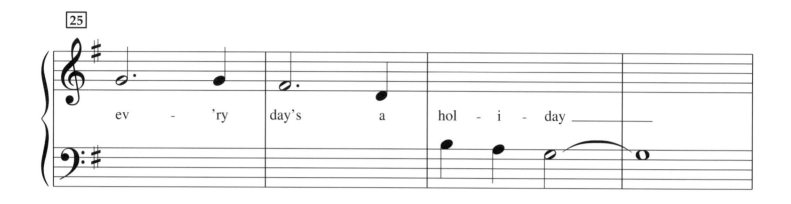
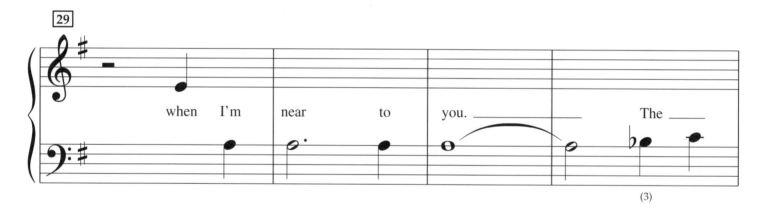
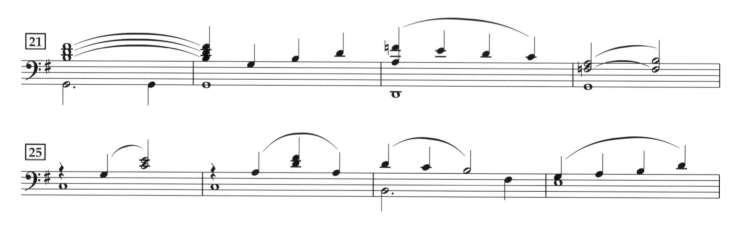

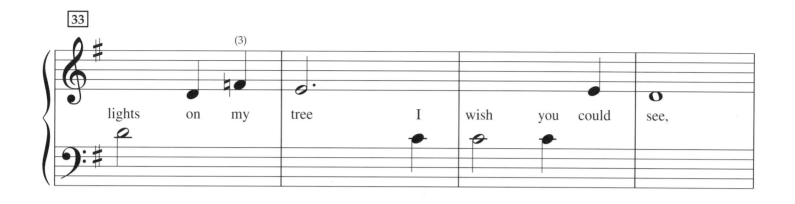
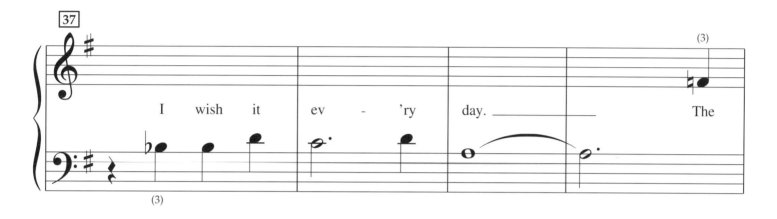
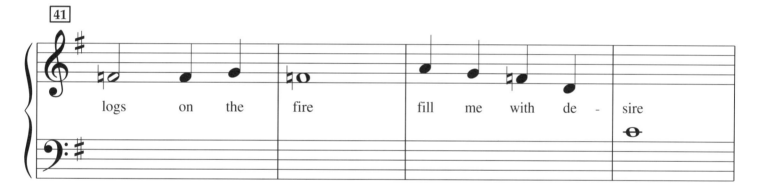

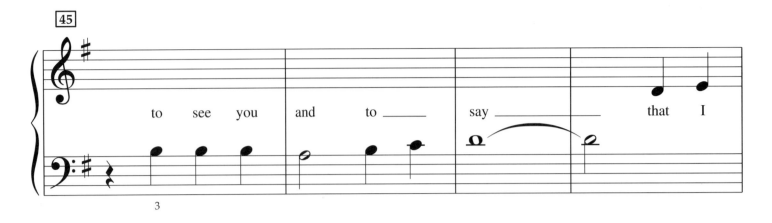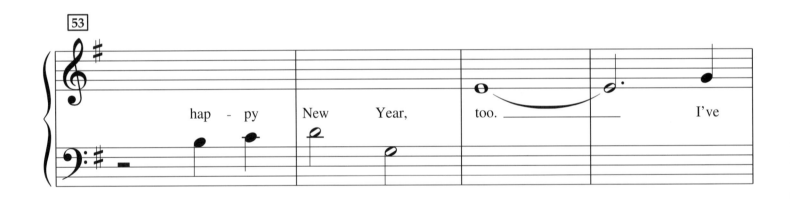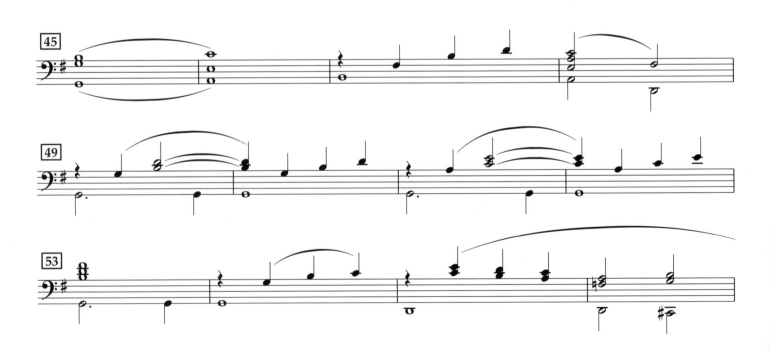

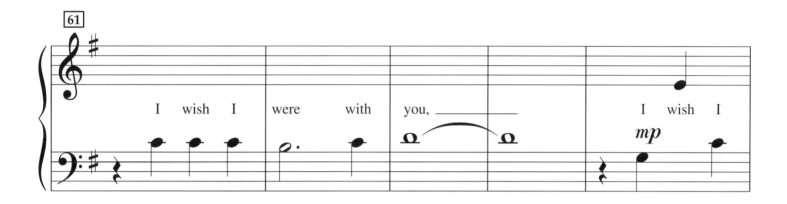
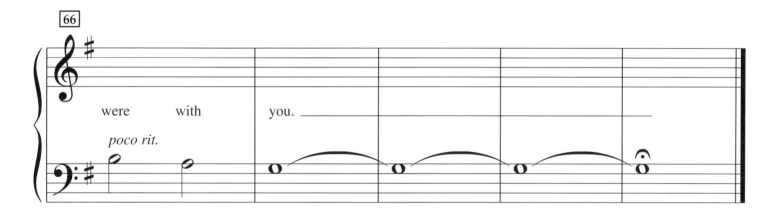
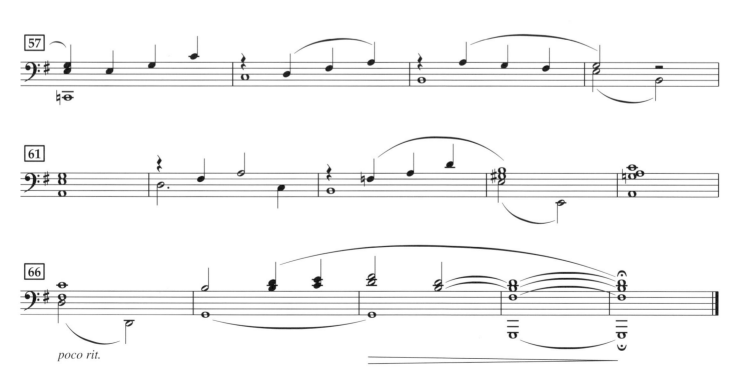

Nuttin' for Christmas

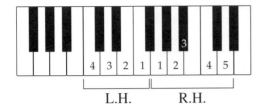

Words and Music by Roy Bennett
and Sid Tepper

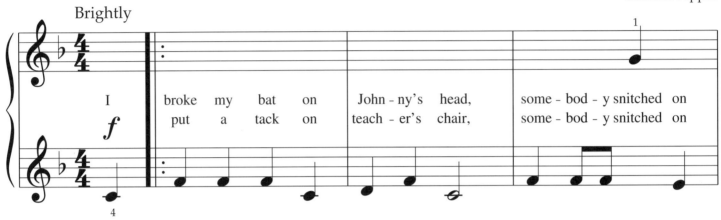

Duet Part (Student plays one octave higher)

Copyright © 1955 by Chappell & Co.
Copyright Renewed
International Copyright Secured   All Rights Reserved

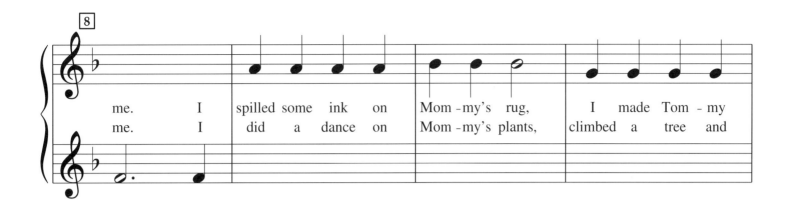
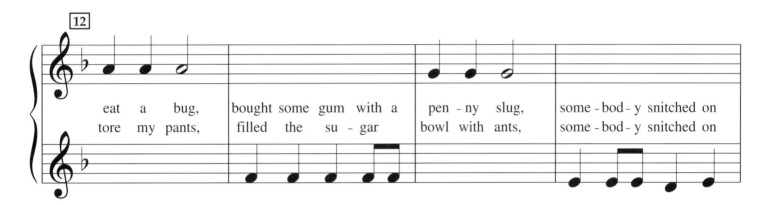
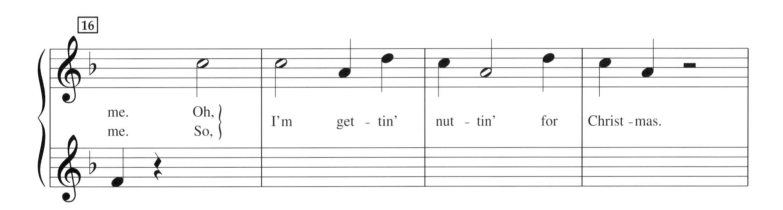

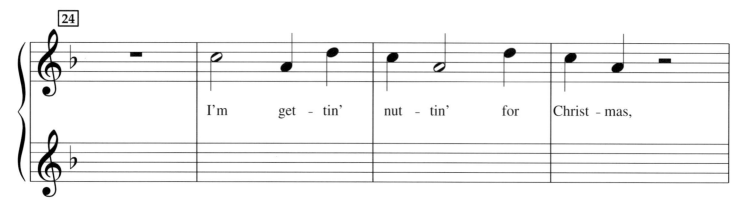
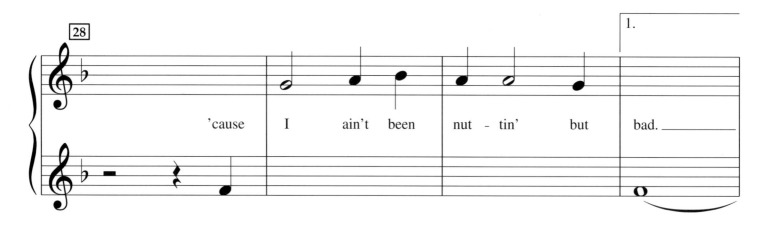

Shake Me I Rattle
(Squeeze Me I Cry)

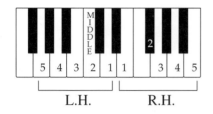

Words and Music by Hal Hackady
and Charles Naylor

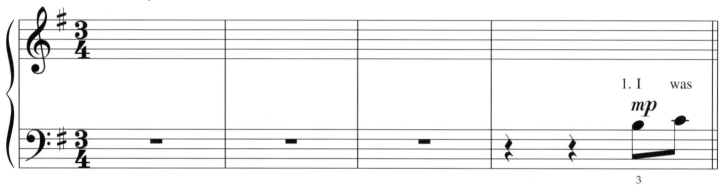

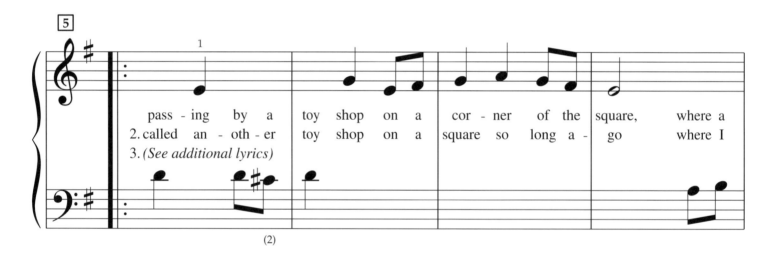

1. passing by a toy shop on a corner of the square, where a
2. called another toy shop on a square so long ago where I
3. *(See additional lyrics)*

Duet Part (Student plays one octave higher than written.)

Copyright © 1957 (Renewed) by Regent Music Corporation (BMI)
International Copyright Secured   All Rights Reserved
Used by Permission

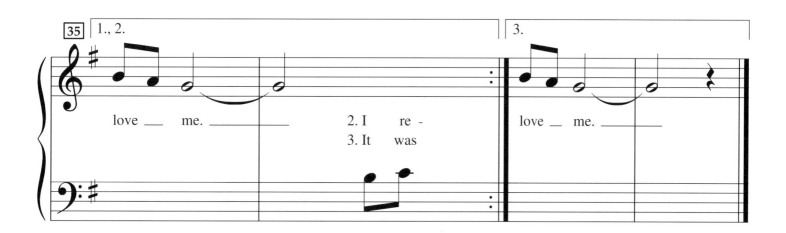

Additional Lyrics

3. It was late and snow was falling as the shoppers hurried by
   Past the girlie at the window with her little head held high.
   They were closing up the toy shop as I hurried thru the door
   Just in time to buy the dolly that her heart was longing for.

   Shake me, I rattle, squeeze me, I cry,
   And I gave her the dolly that we both had longed to buy.
   Shake me, I rattle, squeeze me, I cry.
   Please take me home and love me.

PLAYING PIANO HAS NEVER BEEN EASIER!

5-FINGER PIANO COLLECTIONS FROM HAL LEONARD

BARNEY SONGS
This five-finger piano book features seven Super-Dee-Duper™ songs! Includes: Barney Theme Song • I Love You • Me and My Teddy • My Family's Just Right for Me • The Raindrop Song • Someone to Love You Forever • You Can Count on Me.
_____00316065 ....$7.95

BEATLES! BEATLES!
8 classics, including: A Hard Day's Night • Hey Jude • Love Me Do • P.S. I Love You • Ticket to Ride • Twist and Shout • Yellow Submarine • Yesterday.
_____00292061 ....$7.95

CHURCH SONGS FOR KIDS
Features five-finger arrangements of 15 sacred favorites, including: Amazing Grace • The B-I-B-L-E • Down in My Heart • Fairest Lord Jesus • Hallelu, Hallelujah! • I'm in the Lord's Army • Jesus Loves Me • Kum Ba Yah • My God Is So Great, So Strong and So Mighty • Oh, How I Love Jesus • Praise Him, All Ye Little Children • Zacchaeus and more.
_____00310613 ....$6.95

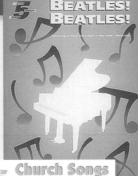

CLASSICAL FAVORITES
arr. Carol Klose

Includes 10 beloved classical pieces from Bach, Bizet, Haydn, Greig and other great composers: Bridal Chorus • Hallelujah! • He Shall Feed His Flock • Largo • Minuet in G • Morning • Rondeau • Surprise Symphony • To a Wild Rose • Toreador Song.
_____00310611 ....$6.95

CONTEMPORARY MOVIE HITS
7 favorite songs from hit films: Go the Distance (Hercules) • My Heart Will Go On (Titanic) • Remember Me This Way (Casper) • Someday (The Hunchback of Notre Dame) • When You Believe (The Prince of Egypt) • You'll Be in My Heart (Tarzan) • You've Got a Friend in Me (Toy Story and Toy Story II).
_____00310687 ....$6.95

DISNEY MOVIE FUN
8 classics, including: Beauty and the Beast • When You Wish Upon a Star • Whistle While You Work • and more.
_____00292067 ....$7.95

DISNEY TUNES
Includes: Can You Feel the Love Tonight? • Chim Chim Cher-ee • Go the Distance • It's a Small World • Supercalifragilisticexpialidocious • Under the Sea • You've Got a Friend in Me • Zero to Hero.
_____00310375 ....$7.95

EENSY WEENSY SPIDER & OTHER NURSERY RHYME FAVORITES
Includes 11 rhyming tunes kids love: Hickory Dickory Dock • Humpty Dumpty • Hush, Little Baby • Jack and Jill • Little Jack Horner • Mary Had a Little Lamb • Peter, Peter Pumpkin Eater • Pop Goes the Weasel • Tom, Tom, the Piper's Son • more.
_____00310465 ....$7.95

GOD BLESS AMERICA®
8 PATRIOTIC AND INSPIRATIONAL SONGS

Features 8 patriotic favorites anyone can play: America, the Beautiful • Battle Hymn of the Republic • God Bless America • My Country, 'Tis of Thee (America) • The Star Spangled Banner • This Is My Country • This Land Is Your Land • You're a Grand Old Flag.
_____00310828 ....$7.95

OUR FAVORITE FOLKSONGS
9 familiar favorites, including: The Blue Tail Fly (aka Jimmy Crack Corn) • Down in the Valley • Oh! Susanna • Yankee Doodle • and more.
_____00310068 ....$5.95

SUPER SILLY SONGS FOR FIVE FINGER PIANO
15 fun songs kids will love to play, including: Animal Fair • Be Kind to Your Web-Footed Friends • Do Your Ears Hang Low? • Little Bunny Foo Foo • The Man on the Flying Trapeze • A Peanut Sat on a Railroad Track • Who Threw the Overalls in Mrs. Murphy's Chowder • and more.
_____00310136 ....$6.95

TV TUNES
Easy arrangements of eight classic theme songs: The Ballad of Davy Crockett • The Brady Bunch • Fraggle Rock Theme • Mickey Mouse March • Mork and Mindy • The Muppet Show Theme • The Odd Couple • Rocky & Bullwinkle.
_____00310666 ....$6.95

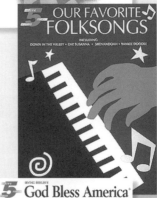

FOR MORE INFORMATION, SEE YOUR LOCAL MUSIC DEALER,
OR WRITE TO:

HAL•LEONARD® CORPORATION
7777 W. BLUEMOUND RD. P.O. BOX 13819 MILWAUKEE, WI 53213

Visit Hal Leonard Online at **www.halleonard.com**

Disney characters and artwork © Disney Enterprises, Inc.

Prices, contents and availability subject to change without notice.

0502